I-SPY

I-SPY PETS
When Human Friendship Is Not Enough

By
SAM JORDISON

HarperCollins*Publishers*
1 London Bridge Street
London SE1 9GF

www.harpercollins.co.uk

First published by HarperCollins*Publishers* 2016

10 9 8 7 6 5 4 3 2 1

A catalogue record of this book is available from the
British Library

ISBN 978-0-00-822073-0

Printed and bound in Spain

MIX
Paper from
responsible sources
FSC™ C007454

FSC™ www.fsc.org

FSC™ is a non-profit international organisation established to promote the
responsible management of the world's forests. Products carrying the FSC
label are independently certified to assure consumers that they come from
forests that are managed to meet the social, economic and ecological needs
of present and future generations, and other controlled sources.

Find out more about HarperCollins and the environment at
www.harpercollins.co.uk/green

The I-SPY concept is simple. It's like the 'I spy with my little eye' game, only instead of all the tedious stuff about 'something beginning with', there are pictures and descriptions and genuine opportunities to use your sleuthing skills to discover interesting things. And laugh at them. It will greatly improve your thus far ignorant life.

Britain is overrun with animals. But so long as you don't venture into town centres on Friday and Saturday nights, you can generally avoid them. Meanwhile, there are also quite a lot of pets to see. They come in all shapes and sizes. It's fun to note down as many different kinds as you can and to gently laugh at just how much they look like their owners. It's also nice to judge people depending on the kind of pets they own. This book will help guide you through that enjoyable process.

You earn a score every time you spot something pictured in the I-SPY books. It's great fun to add up your scores and know that you're doing better than your friends and family.

When your score totals over 250, you're allowed to call yourself an I-SPY Stalwart, second-class honours.

When your score totals over 500, you can write to me, Chief I-SPY, and apply for a special badge.

If you score less than 250, you're a bad doggy and you won't get a treat.

Chief I-SPY, LONDON

Evil Cat

The evil cat is easy to spot because just about every cat on earth is evil*. If human beings demonstrated the same attitude towards the torture of smaller innocent creatures, the same cold disdain for everyone around them and the same delight in killing for sport, the Tory party would never be out of power.

Cats are not your friends! They stay with you only as long as you can offer them food and shelter. When they look at you, they're only trying to work out how easy it would be to eat you, should you die.

*Except your cat. Of course, we know that your cat is purrfect.

I-SPYed on .... **Score**

at .... ⑩

Dog with Pom-poms

In its head, this dog is a proud member of a wild wolf pack, roaming the forests at night under the brilliant moon. In its head, this dog is a hunting machine, a fierce fighter and an unfuckable-with warrior. In its head, this dog is a king. On its head, it has a fluffy little hat with pom-poms.

I-SPYed on .... Score

at .... (30)

Dog and Phone

'Dog and bone' is Cockney rhyming slang for telephone. An actual dog and a phone, meanwhile, is rhyming slang for all alone, and alas, possibly also loser. Because if you've dressed your dog up and taken a photo of him looking like he's talking on the telephone, I'm afraid that things are not going as well in your life as they could be. The good news is that you have a dog, and the lovely little fellow probably thinks the world of you and will enjoy going for a nice walk right about now. The bad news is everything else. Oh well. At least you got a funny photo.

I-SPYed on .... **Score**

at .... **(20)**

Embarrassing Collar

Sometimes pets have unfortunate incidents and their
owners have to make them wear a special collar in
case they start trying to lick their nether regions. This
treatment is always necessary, even though the pet will
find it deeply embarrassing, as this picture shows.
(The dog looks pretty upset about his collar too.)

I-SPYed on .... **Score**

at .... (**10**)

Bunny Rabbits

These children are happy right now, but later their
rabbits will be cooked with white wine, olive oil, garlic,
a sprig of rosemary, a couple of bay leaves, an onion,
a carrot, a sprinkle of flour, pepper and the salt from
their tears.

I-SPYed on .... **Score**

at .... **(30)**

If you can catch and eat your own rabbit,
score 50 points.

I-SPYed on .... **Score**

at .... **(50)**

Innuendo Cat

There was once a brighter, kinder age when it was possible to get through a week without hearing lewd jokes. Alas, those days are gone. Good spies should try to stopper their ears against any cat-related filth.

I-SPYed on .... Score

at .... (**-20**)

Stoner Dog

Maan! There was this one time in 1967, oh boy. It was because of Jerry and the Dead, really. I think I was just stood there for 12 hours and who knows where the kids had gone. I thought I was this, like, mote of dust in God's eye and everything was glowing and it was, just, totally, where was I? Oh yeah. How do you like my new freakin' duds, man? Check out the chick behind me, too. We roll like this all the time, man. I gotta tell you about this one time in 1967, oh boy. It was because of Jerry and the Dead, really...

I-SPYed on .... **Score**

at .... **(30)**

Dog with Waterproof Accessory

Look! This dog's owner has invented an upside-down umbrella for him. Sometimes you might see dogs wearing special dog-shaped outdoor coats, too. You can also score points if you see them wearing fancy Spanish Civil War-style bandanas. As you note down your points, remember to judge the owners harshly – to mutter under your breath that the dog's already got its own coat and to think cruel thoughts about how if you want to dress up a small, ugly creature, you really should just produce or adopt a human baby.

I-SPYed on .... Score

at .... (25)

Dog on a Trailer

Owners have all kinds of interesting and unusual ways of transporting their pets! If you're very lucky, you may see one on a specially made motorbike trailer – although the scene in this particular picture will never be recreated. Twenty seconds after it was taken, the lady in the pink shirt kicked off the bike stand, pulled on the accelerator and screamed off into the distance, shouting that now she was finally going to have some 'fun'.

The dog briefly tried to cling on to the roof of that weird house-thing with his teeth, but was forced to let go as gravity pulled him backwards, backwards and rolling, rolling and bumping, bumping and flying over the hard tarmac. Miraculously, he escaped with no injuries other than those to his pride. The man, meanwhile, didn't move an inch. He's still there today, in exactly the same position. A family of robins have made their home in his pockets and crows sometimes come to perch on his left hand.

Life is strange, in all kinds of ways.

I-SPYed on .... **Score**

at .... (**40**)

Frightening Sheep

Most I-SPYers probably assume that they could take a sheep on. But most probably haven't actually tried. Until you've been there, just you and the sheep – oh God. Those weird, staring eyes. Those stamping feet. The impossibility of making the beast see reason. That surprising speed and unexpected anger... Just don't drop your I-SPY book as you run away. These points have been hard earned!

In truth, the miracle is that we get to eat sheep rather than the other way round. As soon as sheep get together and really start thinking things through, we're doomed. Mankind's dominion will end. Mint sauce will have new and frightening uses.

I-SPYed on .... Score

at .... (**30**)

BEWARE OF THE SHEEP

The Dog Who Looks Just Like Its Owner

It's fun to see a dog who looks just like her owner.
It's nice to laugh at subconscious human vanity and to
marvel at the vagaries of fate. Just don't dwell on the
similarities for too long. Don't think about how deep
they go.

The saddest thing about the dog in this picture, for
instance, is that it too is a chronic wineaholic. It tells
itself that rather than being an addict, it's a connoisseur,
because the sauce it quaffs costs £15 a bottle and
comes from an unpronounceable region of France.

I-SPYed on .... **Score**

at .... (**10**)

The Surrogate Child

'Would 'ee like to have a little chocolate? Likkle bit of chocky can't hurt 'im. Oooh. Who's a good boy? Did 'ee like it? Is his chops all messy now? Give us a kiss. Ooooh. No tongues! That's better. Such a good boy. Who loves 'im? Mummy and Daddy will give you some more treats later. Okay. Just one more. Now. If he's good. There! One more kiss, too? Who loves you? Oh. Does 'ee need to do a poo-poo? Not yet! Oh naughty boy! Oh well. Mummy and Daddy will clear it up.'

I-SPYed on .... **Score**

at .... (**10**)

Massive Man, Really Small Bird

It's lovely to see great big men with tiny birds.
It always raises so many interesting questions.

I-SPYed on .... Score

at .... (30)

Bad Dogs

You'll sometimes see pets that have been
weaponised by their owners. They're big, strong,
have great mouthfuls of teeth and snarls, and they're
nearly always angry. Boiling-in-their-eyes angry.
So damn angry. Angry because they know that their
owners have embarrassingly small penises.

I·SPYed on .... **Score**

at .... ⑩

Sometimes the bad dog will turn on its owner instead
of attacking innocent punters. There is a special
German word for this situation: *schadenfreude*.

I·SPYed on .... **Score**

at .... ㊿

Useless Pet

There are a lot of goldfish in the world but they're really hard to I-SPY. Not only do you have to go into someone else's house to see them, but the fish must still be alive by the time you get there.

I-SPYed on .... Score

at .... (40)

Is there clearly too much food floating on top of the poor fish's water? Is it swimming in barely aerated toxic sludge? Has its water turned brown? That's great! You can score an extra 50 points!

I-SPYed on .... Score

at .... (50)

YouTube Star

Pets are often expensive. They demand daily grooming and nutrition. Vet bills are painful. Our animal companions also have the unfortunate tendency to chew furniture, smash into vases and eat important pieces of post.
It's only fair that they should work, too. And what better way to make money than to dress them in a funny outfit, make them run around in frantic circles, whip out your iPhone and post the video on social media?

Okay. There are infinitely easier ways to make money. Your pet will never become a YouTube star, and even if it does, someone else will nick the video and take all the ad revenue. But that doesn't seem to stop anyone. Go to most parks in Britain and you'll see people frantically trying to pap their own pets. And you'll score some lovely I-SPY points in the process.

I-SPYed on.. **Score**

at 10

Dog in a Bag

Four legs: good. Two legs: better. Not using your legs
at all because your owner has forgotten that you're
a living creature rather than a fashion accessory:
better still!

Since the beginning of time, pretty much all that
dogs have ever wanted is to go for a nice stroll outside.
Even hearing the word 'walk' is enough to send some of
them into paroxysms of delight and excited anticipation.
To say that they love to go out and stretch their legs is as
obvious as pointing out that the sun is quite hot, grass
is green and politicians might not always tell the truth.
So when you see a dog in a bag, you see the death of all
their doggy dreams.

I-SPYed on.. **Score**

at .... **(20)**

The Small Dog Syndrome

This kind of dog is very easy to I-SPY because it will attack you as soon as it sees you. No matter that it's smaller than your foot, and if you were so minded you could hoof it into next week with one well-aimed kick. Teeth bared, eyes sparking, furiously yapping, it will charge right at you, for reasons even it doesn't understand. It's also the terror of Alsatians, Bulldogs and Rottweilers. But don't let that trick you into thinking it has any redeeming qualities. It's a little arsehole.

I-SPYed on.. Score

at .... (10)

The Best Friend

This man likes his dog more than his wife. Or his children.
Or his brothers. Or the memory of his parents. Or his
colleagues. Or anyone he has ever met ever. Seriously,
this man *likes* his dog. Much more than he likes you.

I-SPYed on.. **Score**

at .... (15)

See the man who likes his dog hold a fully engaged and
sustained philosophical conversation with his furry friend.

I-SPYed on.. **Score**

at .... (25)

See the dog answer back and start discussing
Heisenberg's uncertainty principle.

I-SPYed on.. **Score**

at .... (75)

Pub Dog

The sign of a really good pub is a really good dog sitting in a corner by the fire. Or better still, a really good dog working the room. Pub dogs are better than any Zen master when it comes to dishing out good vibes. They can expertly navigate even the most crowded bars without getting under anyone's feet and radiate a Grade Ten force field of chilled benevolence as they go.

When you see them, the pub dog will make you feel great, popping by your table just long enough for a quick pat, ear ruffle and whispered 'good boy'. And then, on they plod, back into the throng, calmly emanating wisdom. They're quiet saints of the cheery night, the spirit of real ale made flesh. They're the best.

Just make sure you aren't anywhere near them when they fart.

I-SPYed on.. **Score**

at .... (**25**)

Work out who the pub dog actually belongs to.

I-SPYed on.. **Score**

at .... (**50**)

Scary Cat

Do. Not. Fuck. With. The. Scary. Cat.

You might think that you're bigger than the Scary Cat.
You might think that you're faster than the Scary Cat.
You might think that you're cleverer than the Scary Cat.
But you seriously overestimate your chances.

There's nothing tougher than a tough cat and nothing
meaner. It will play dirtier, smarter and crueller than you.
It will get your face and your eyes with its claws. Even its
hiss will make your balls retreat right back into your body.
Just write down your points and run away. You don't stand
a chance.

I-SPYed on... **Score**

at... **(30)**

See the Scary Cat humiliate a dog and award yourself
50 extra points.

I-SPYed on... **Score**

at... **(50)**

The Creepy Pet

In order to I-SPY this kind of pet, you'll probably have to
go round to its owner's house. This may prove difficult.
Not least because the owner is likely to be an unholy
freak. They may try to tell you that their lizard
is interesting, that their snake is clever or that their
spider is an astonishingly skilled hunter. They may even
try to suggest that touching its horrible hard skin and
looking into those cold, cruel reptile eyes is fulfilling.
But there will always be the suspicion that they're serial
killers and they only like these horrible creatures because
they remind them of pain and death. Get in, get your
I-SPY points and get out fast!

I-SPYed on .... **Score**

at .... **(50)**

Dead Pet

Your furry friend's last job is to give you and your children a useful lesson about mortality and moving on. Sadly, this lesson mainly involves teaching you just how much death sucks. Life may be a piece of shit, when you look at it, but it's far better than the alternative. It's better still when shared with a friend who can't answer back or disagree with you about the Labour Party.

However, there is some good news about pet death! If you lose your best buddy, it does mean that you can have the joy of finding a new one and starting all over again. There's nothing nicer than a puppy, after all.

I-SPYed on.. **Score**

at .... (**20**)

Find a dead creature splatted by the side of the road.

I-SPYed on.. **Score**

at .... (**30**)

Awesome Pet

It's fun to laugh at our four-legged friends and their owners. But it's even more fun to actually hang out with them. Cats are cool. Dogs are doting. Rabbits are sweet. Even goldfish can briefly distract you from the crushing reality of mortality and the horror of being all alone on this overheating rock, spinning purposelessly around a dying sun in an unfathomably large galaxy, lost in the cold, vast, dark emptiness of space...

There's nothing more joyful than a Labrador plunging into water. There are few finer sights than a Spaniel going full tilt after a flying tennis ball. There's nothing more warming to the heart than the sound of a big Collie's tail thumping the floor in joy at your return from a hard day at work.

Pets are wonderful. It's a reward just to see them.
As well as the easiest 20 I-SPY points you'll ever make.

I-SPYed on... **Score**

at .... **(20)**

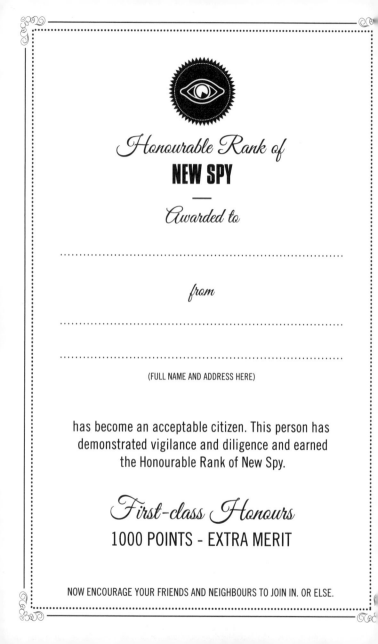

Honourable Rank of
NEW SPY

—

Awarded to

....

from

....

....

(FULL NAME AND ADDRESS HERE)

has become an acceptable citizen. This person has
demonstrated vigilance and diligence and earned
the Honourable Rank of New Spy.

First-class Honours
1000 POINTS - EXTRA MERIT

NOW ENCOURAGE YOUR FRIENDS AND NEIGHBOURS TO JOIN IN. OR ELSE.